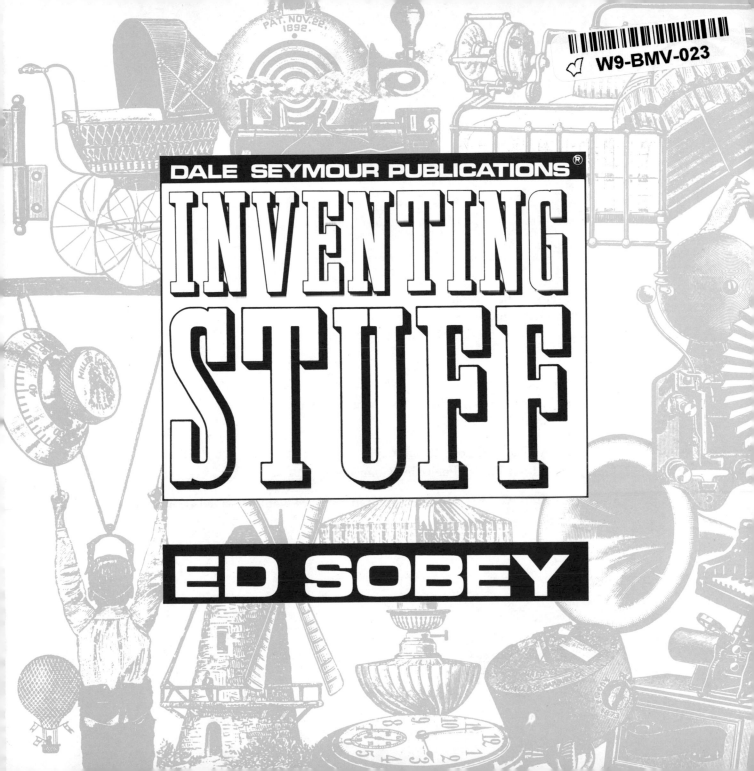

DALE SEYMOUR PUBLICATIONS®

INVENTING STUFF

ED SOBEY

Project Editor: Joan Gideon
Production: Leanne Collins
Text and Cover Design: Maryann Murphy

Many of the designations used by manufacturers and sellers to distinguish their products are claimed as trademarks. Where those designations appear in this book, they have been printed in initial caps.

Published by Dale Seymour Publications®, an imprint of the Alternative Publishing Group of Addison-Wesley Publishing Company.

Order Number   21357

ISBN 0-86651-937-8

5 6 7 8 9 10-ML-04 03 02 01 00

DALE
SEYMOUR
PUBLICATIONS®
P.O. BOX 10888
PALO ALTO, CA 94303

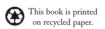
This book is printed
on recycled paper.

CONTENTS

INTRODUCTION

A Note to Parents and Teachers

Kids Inventing? Absolutely!

Kids are natural inventors. They are at the most creative stage in their lives, and they are filled with creative ideas. But inventing is more than *having* creative ideas. Inventing is *using* those creative ideas to solve problems.

This book encourages young people—especially those in grades 6 through 9—to use their creative talents to invent solutions to problems. For teenagers and even younger children, expressing their creativity through a new device or toy can be richly rewarding. Whether they invent new games and toys, or devices for cleaning up after their pets, or ways to take out the garbage, or any of thousands of other gizmos—the most important thing is that they are taking the time to think—to ponder, to tinker, to experiment, to play with ideas, to stretch their minds.

Living in the information age, we often feel the pressure to pour gallons of data daily into the heads of our growing children. But people don't learn that way. They learn best by thinking and working things out for themselves. When kids invent, the process of inventing motivates them to learn. It will give them countless hours of exploration and fun. It will give them the technological self-confidence to survive in a technological world, and it will help them learn how to think and solve problems.

Inventing at School and at Home

Every day, at some time during the day, children must be given a chance to think for themselves. If school is merely the process of memorizing what the teacher said or what appears in the textbook, kids are losing an opportunity to think. Even hands-on activities won't do the trick if they follow a cookbook approach—because there is no room to think here, either. Any time an activity is *coached* or *directed,* someone else is doing the lion's share of the thinking.

Furthermore, kids need the chance to exercise their creative powers in technical fields. Typically their main exposure to creativity is in writing and the arts. Science is rarely presented as a creative field—and thus many creative students opt out of science as soon as they can. Increasingly, though, educational researchers are suggesting the types of thinking outlined in this book as an alternative to the traditional school approach. Science curriculums are being revised to reduce the time spent in rote learning and to add inquiry-based exploration. This makes good sense, as scientists and inventors of all ages learn this way.

Outside of school, young people typically experience a lot of demands on their time—soccer practice, music lessons, dance and art classes, scout troops, gymnastics, and so on. And then, when they're finally home, there's the ubiquitous television and video games. But suppose families set aside just half an hour a day for the kids to ponder, to tinker, to think, and to create. If you set them up with this book and access to materials for tinkering, your children may soon discover that creating something is inherently more fun than watching TV—with lots more payoffs.

Inventing motivates people to work longer and harder on a project, as they pursue their creative ideas to make them work. Learning occurs when thoughtful time is spent on a task. Inventing is learning at its most effective, because it establishes the need and desire to know and understand. This is not contrived learning without relevance to the children's world. This is learning to solve a problem that confronts them.

Some teachers are discovering the excitement of getting their classes—or individual students, or small groups—involved in special activities like the national Odyssey of the Mind and Science Olympiad competitions. Districts here and there have set up their own versions of these challenging events, which typically involve students in team-oriented, problem-solving and risk-taking activities, such as light bulb or egg drops, building with straws or balsa wood, performing on original musical instruments, floating pennies on foil rafts, and a host of other problem situations designed to stretch young minds. Often parents are engaged as mentors and coaches.

While teachers and families alike may encourage students to participate actively in such events, rarely is there any provision made to *practice* for them. Urging students to undertake the kinds of inventive thinking and tinkering suggested in *Inventing Stuff* is one good way to prepare them for the sort of creative noodling that ensures a successful and enjoyable experience in these creative competitions.

Who Is This Book For?

Is this a book for boys? Yes—and for girls, too. Creative and inventive ability are not gender specific. Although the history of invention is dominated by males, the future of invention need not be. We all have to work a little harder to overcome social hindrances to ensure that girls have the same opportunities and encouragement as boys do.

Anyone who enjoys working with their hands will especially enjoy the challenges here. Many kids learn by *doing,* and in too many classrooms they are expected to learn primarily through *listening.* Youngsters with intelligent, active minds, who learn by doing instead of listening, will especially enjoy this book—and they will learn through their experiences. In addition to the technical knowledge they gain, they'll be learning things like muscular coordination, use of tools, thinking skills, and, if they are working with other children, teamwork.

The academically precocious will likely find the ideas challenging. However, for some it will be frustrating, and purposely so. This book doesn't provide the answers, or even all the details to copy the suggested projects. We don't want kids to *copy*; we want them to *invent.*

The book's seven chapters offer a variety of approaches to the inventing process. "You Are an Inventor," is a way to help kids see themselves through new eyes as they are introduced to the notion of inventing. Teachers will welcome the next chapter, "Your Idea Factory"— it has great mental warm-ups that are an easy way to get creative thinking activities into the classroom routine. "Inventing Backwards," can inspire a host of great at-home projects. "Invent by Solving Problems" walks the reader through the inventing process and can serve as a good in-class introduction to independent projects. "Invent by Finding New Uses for Things" and "Projects for Creative Tinkering" are both filled with ideas to turn to when kids don't seem able to get started on their own. And "Making Your Inventions Pay Off" answers the question, "Now I've invented something—what can I do with it?"

How to Nurture Young Inventors

No matter how you choose to use this book, there are six specific actions you can take to encourage young inventors.

1. Give them freedom. No one can invent if someone is always providing directions, telling them what to do. You can help them get started on a project, but then *back off*. Of course, you can provide assistance when it is needed and asked for. However, don't do anything for them that they could do for themselves.

If you are working on a project together, don't take over. Let the kids come up with their own ideas and solutions, and then let them do as much of the fabrication as possible. A test of your effectiveness is to stop in the midst of the project and assess who is doing the work. If *you* are working like a beaver and the kids are sitting doing nothing, or are slinking away, you are doing too much.

Even more important, give them the freedom to fail, and to make mistakes. Failure is inherent in inventing. It occurs, and you should expect it. In fact, it's a key part of how inventors learn. Each failure provides one more stepping stone to eventual success. Treat failures as a part of the process, and encourage your young inventors to keep at it. Perseverance is what separates successful from unsuccessful inventors.

Freedom to explore, of course, does not mean throwing all caution to the wind. You need to exercise caution whenever young people are learning to use tools, and you should supervise especially closely if they are using 110-volt electricity.

2. Give them time to tinker. Rome wasn't built in a day. Adult scientists and inventors need time to develop their ideas, and so do kids—time to think, and wonder, and play with ideas. Don't expect them to finish a project in an hour, or a day, or as overnight homework. Let the project stretch out over several days or even weeks. If a project has engaged their interest, they will return happily to it day after day.

If they hit a snag, encourage them to keep at it. Let them grind on a problem; don't jump in to solve it. Struggling with a problem is an important part of the inventing process. Often the best inventions arise from a protracted struggle.

3. Encourage questions. Nothing is more important for learning than questioning. Questions show thought, creativity, and curiosity. Each one of the hundred questions that may bombard you each day is an opening into the child's mind, and an opportunity for you to encourage learning. Each one deserves all the attention that you can muster.

To encourage questions, ponder them yourself. Ask questions in return. Reframing the question can sometimes help the child understand. Go together to a resource such as an encyclopedia or a library. Many questions are answered best by doing an experiment or trying an invention. Work together on these to satisfy their curiosity and yours.

No teacher or parent can provide adequate answers to all questions. So don't try. It's OK to say, "I don't know." But don't stop there. Ponder the question and help search for an answer. Also, let young people see you asking and finding answers to questions of your own. In this way, you are modeling the behavior you want to encourage.

4. Give positive feedback. Undoubtedly, the output of kids' efforts will not look like a commercially made product, and they will be keenly aware of this themselves. If you rave too much about the product, your praises may ring false. It's better to compliment them sincerely on their ingenuity, on their hard work, on their perseverance.

The product may be quite impractical, even unusable. (Then again, it *could* have great value, and you're simply not seeing it.) You can always laud their creativity and challenge them to "see if it will work."

Encourage them to make working models of their inventions. What looks good on paper may not work at all in three dimensions. This is part of the learning process. Help them bounce back from disappointments, and suggest that they give it another try.

Of course, negative feedback will drain their enthusiasm, leading to frustration and quite possibly the end of their efforts. Your heartfelt compliments, continuing interest, and encouragement will be the most important rewards for them. Additional prizes or gifts are probably not necessary.

5. Encourage them to complete the project. Not *all* projects need to be completed, but at least some should be seen through to a final stage. You may want to establish a target (but not a deadline) for completion. Suggest that the finished project could be shown to a visiting relative or friend who will offer positive feedback. Or suggest that they enter it in an invention contest. Help your child understand that although not all projects need to be completed, the completed ones will bring them the most praise and rewards.

6. Give them exposure to ideas outside the home and classroom. Take them on a walk through the woods, or visit a factory, or a museum. Each activity should be an adventure in which everyone tries to see things you haven't seen before. But keep in mind that for most young people, just *seeing* objects isn't much fun, especially if the objects are behind glass. Nor does it provide much learning.

Doing is how kids learn. Take them places where they can touch things, do things, try things. In these environments, let *them* set the pace of discovery and the length of visit. Although you may feel the urge to "see it all," they may want to spend the entire visit working on one activity. That's good. Let them do it.

Most books aim to provide you with all you need to know on a subject. This one aims higher—it aims to open minds. This is not the definitive book of invention. It is an incubator of ideas and projects whose scope and diversity will go far beyond the imagination of the author. *Inventing Stuff* is intended to be the start, not the end.

With your help, inventing can become one of your students' or children's favorite activities. Let's make that happen.

YOU ARE
AN INVENTOR

Have you ever thought of yourself as an inventor? You are one.

You are an inventor every time you come up with a new solution to a problem. Inventors are people who solve problems.

Inventors often solve problems by making machines. Take the Wright brothers, for example. They are known as inventors of an early airplane—but really, they solved two problems: how to use an engine to push their plane fast enough to fly, and how to make the plane turn without crashing. When they designed devices to solve these problems, their plane flew.

Inventors sometimes solve problems by discovering new ways to do things. Robert R. Williams worked for many years to find a way to make vitamin B_1. He didn't *invent* vitamin B_1—it is found naturally in some of the food we eat. But Williams did invent a way to make the vitamin in a factory. His invention has helped thousands of people who don't get enough B_1 in their food. Every other vitamin pill and the medicines we take when we're sick were also discovered by inventors.

If you have ever made an original device, or made up a new toy or game, or if you have found a new way to make something, you are an inventor. You are surrounded by things

that people have invented. Complex machines like radios, televisions, and automobiles have hundreds or thousands of parts. Each of these was invented by someone.

Look for the little printing that's often on the back or bottom of toys or tools. Some will have a *patent number*. For example, on a Wham-O Frisbee flying disc, you will find printed: U.S. PAT. NO. 3,354,678. The number comes from the U.S. Patent and Trademark Office, a government agency. It means that the toy is an original invention and should not be copied by anyone else. See if you can find patent numbers on other things in your house.

WHAT CAN YOU INVENT?

You know that you can invent because you can solve problems. You solve problems every day. Suppose you can't reach a glass in the cabinet. You can figure out how to get one, and solve the problem. Of course, you don't always *invent* when you solve problems. One solution might be to drag a chair over to stand on. That would be solving the problem, but not inventing. If, instead, you built a long-handled gripper to grab glasses on high shelves, *that* would be an invention. When you solve a problem by making something new, you are inventing.

Could you invent a new rocket for the space program? Probably not, unless you are a rocket scientist. People invent things that solve problems they are familiar with. If you know all about rockets, then you might invent a better one. But even if you are not (yet) a rocket scientist, there are hundreds of opportunities for you to invent—in your home and at school.

How do you find a problem that *is* something you might be able to solve with an invention? Just ask. Everyone has problems. Some are really big problems that are very difficult to solve. Some are small problems that are easier to solve.

HOW OLD IS THAT PATENT?

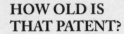

When you find a patent number, look to see how big the number is. The first patent in this country was issued in 1790. By 1992, 5 million patents had been issued. Each patent number is issued in numerical order. So if you find one that is larger than 5 million, it was patented after March 1992. If you find one that is smaller than 1 million, it marks something that was invented before this century. Today about 100,000 patents are issued each year. So, you can estimate from the patent number approximately when a product was patented. About when was the Frisbee patented?

What problems do you have? Does someone in your house play a radio too loud? Do you have to clean up after your pets? Or take out the smelly garbage? These are problems that you might be able to solve with inventions. The more familiar you are with the problem, the better able you will be to invent a good solution. Look for problems all around you in your daily life.

PORTRAIT OF AN INVENTOR

Lots of different kinds of people are inventors, but they all share certain traits. See if you fit the "portrait" of an inventor described here.

You are curious

All inventors are curious. They constantly look for new and unusual things. They like to look inside things to see how they work. They ask lots of questions.

Asking questions is very important. You may not always get answers, but you can learn a lot just by asking. Ask the people around you lots of questions. It's fun to see what people know, what they don't know, and what they think they know.

When you come up with a *very* good question, one without an easy answer, write it down and put it in an idea file. (We will talk more about idea files in the next chapter.)

Sometimes you can get answers by asking a person who has some expertise. Sometimes you can get answers by looking up information in books, like an encyclopedia, or by calling the information desk at your library. But sometimes you just won't be able to find the answer to your question. Then you might want to try an experiment—curious people love to experiment.

You love to work on your ideas

Inventors tinker. They play with their ideas and their inventions. They try different ways of doing things.

Suppose you're trying to solve a problem. Often the first idea you have doesn't work very well. So, you have to tinker. You think some more about your idea, and you ask yourself questions. "Why doesn't it work better? How can I make it better?"

Sometimes just playing with your invention will give you great ideas. Tinkering, while asking yourself lots of questions, is the best way to come up with good inventions.

WHAT'S THIS STUFF?

Dr. Roy Plunkett was a chemist doing experiments. One day his experiment did not come out the way he expected it to. Instead of starting over, he asked lots of questions. What was the strange powder inside his glass tubes? Why would nothing stick to it? And what could it be used for? Dr. Plunkett had invented Teflon, a substance now used inside some pans to keep food from sticking. It has lots of other uses, too. Teflon was discovered when someone who was curious kept asking questions.

WHAT MADE IT MELT?

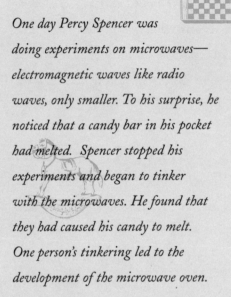

One day Percy Spencer was doing experiments on microwaves— electromagnetic waves like radio waves, only smaller. To his surprise, he noticed that a candy bar in his pocket had melted. Spencer stopped his experiments and began to tinker with the microwaves. He found that they had caused his candy to melt. One person's tinkering led to the development of the microwave oven.

You can stick with a tough problem

Inventors are persistent. If you are persistent, it means that you stick to the job. You don't give up.

Inventing is not easy. There are lots of problems to solve, and if you give up because there is a tough problem, you won't invent. Maybe you've worked for a long time on what seemed like a great idea—but it just won't work. You don't give up on the problem. Instead, you look for a different solution. Or, you may try to get some help. But you don't give up.

Each time you try an idea, you are learning something useful. If it doesn't work, don't think of it as a "mistake" or a "failure." Each try is leading you closer to success by showing you what doesn't work.

You proudly share your work

The greatest inventors share their inventions with the world. You are not finished with the process when you have your invention working. To be really successful, you need to share it.

Inventing isn't just making a new device or process. When you show it to others, they can learn and be inspired. You get acknowledgment for your invention. And, if yours is a very good invention, you may get a prize or payment for it. Don't leave your invention in the laboratory. Share it. This may mean selling your idea to a toy or game company that will manufacture it. It may mean submitting your idea to an invention contest. Or it may simply mean showing your idea to your parents, to your friends, or to your teachers.

One way of sharing your invention is to get a patent for it. Getting a patent does two things: it protects your idea, so someone else won't steal it, and it shows the world how you solved a problem. This can help other inventors. Someone else may take your solution and use it on a different problem to make a new invention. The patent system helps people share ideas.

FOUR WAYS TO INVENT

Inventing seems very hard at first. If you just sit down to think up a new invention, you may not think of anything at all.

Most inventions don't start that way. Inventors usually get their ideas while they are tinkering with something already made, or when they see ways to do something just a little bit better.

Very few inventions are completely new ideas. The car was really just an improvement on the carriage pulled by horses. The gasoline engine replaced the horse. Even

1,800 BRIGHT IDEAS

You probably know that Thomas Edison invented the light bulb. You may not know how long he worked to do it. Edison tried more than 1,800 different ways to make a really bright and long-lasting bulb before he found one that would really work. Think of it this way: Edison was probably the most successful inventor of all time, but he made more than 1,800 mistakes on one project. Today we remember Edison for his one successful solution for the light bulb. Maybe we should remember him more for his persistence.

WHEN YOUR IDEAS ARE IGNORED

When you share a new idea, don't expect everyone to recognize your genius immediately. Sometimes it takes a long time. Consider the copy machine. Nearly every office or school in America now has at least one copy machine. Where would we be without them? Believe it or not, it was many years before the inventor could get any company interested in making copiers. Chester Carlson invented the dry-copy process in 1938. He showed it to more than 20 companies. Not one believed that it was a good invention. It took him 9 years to sell his idea, and then 11 more years before the first copier went on the market. Coming up with the invention, by itself, didn't make Carlson a successful inventor. He had to solve lots of other problems in order to share his invention with the world.

18

the light bulb was not new. Inventors had already found ways to create light from electricity. Edison just worked on improvements to make a useful product.

So how do inventors invent? Here are four ways.

1. Make improvements

Many inventions are improvements on earlier inventions. Elisha Otis didn't invent elevators. He invented the automatic brake for elevators, making them safe enough for people to use. People were afraid of using elevators until he invented the elevator brake. Otis made an improvement in an existing device.

Dustbusters are small, portable vacuum cleaners. They are useful for quick spot clean-ups, and for cleaning car interiors. Many have been sold under this trade name; similar miniature vacuums are also on the market. But regular-sized vacuums have been around for a long time. The miniature version is just a modification of an older invention, using a battery instead of household electricity.

You are surrounded by hundreds of gadgets and machines. Do they always work the way you want them to? If you can figure a way to make one of them work better, you may have an invention. Start looking.

2. Make combinations

Some inventions are combinations of two or more other inventions. One good example is the telephone answering machine—a combination of a telephone and an audio tape recorder. Another example is the clock radio—the combination of an electric clock and a radio.

Can you think of two inventions that would make a new product if you combined them? Try making a list. Write down all the household appliances or garden tools you can think of. Then start combining them in pairs. Most of the combinations will be silly, like combining a shovel and a dishwasher. But maybe you can find a combination that could work.

3. Make breakthroughs

Most inventions are not completely new ideas—but some are. These are called *breakthrough inventions*. The photocopier is one example. Before the photocopier, there was no way to make copies instantly.

Most breakthrough inventions grow out of trying to solve a problem. So, if you want to make a breakthrough, you need a list of problems. Start by listing problems that you personally have. Ask your friends what really bugs them, and add their problems to your list. (Things like "doing homework" or "little brothers" probably shouldn't go on the list—your solutions might get you into trouble!)

Over time, keep adding to your list of problems. One of the most important things for an inventor is having the right problem to solve. Look at your list from time to time to see if a good idea jumps out at you. Your problem list may give you great ideas.

MENTAL WARM-UP

Sometimes it helps to warm up your creative powers before you try to work them hard. There are lots of warm-ups you can try. Here is one type. Make a list of all the uses you can think of for a particular object. For example, how many uses can you come up with for a hammer? Sure it can drive nails, but could it also hold down papers, hold open a door, or be a piece of art?

Can you come up with 10 other uses? How about 100? Get your friends together and try this type of mental warm-up with them.

4. Use mistakes

Everyone *makes* mistakes. Inventors *use* them. Many inventions have come from mistakes. What's key here is to be curious about mistakes and to see what made them mistakes.

Charles Goodyear spilled rubber mixed with sulfur onto a hot stove. Most people would have cleaned up the mess and been angry at themselves. Instead, Goodyear tinkered with the mistake and learned that he had invented vulcanization, the process that makes rubber usable in hundreds of products.

You cannot control when a "good" mistake will occur. However, you *can* be ready for it. When a mistake happens, ask questions. Try to understand what happened and what you can learn from it. That's the secret of turning mistakes into successes.

By now it should be clear to you that you *can* invent. You know what traits make a good inventor. And you know some different ways to approach inventing. So what are you waiting for? Let's get started.

YOUR
IDEA FACTORY

Your brain can do incredible things. It can remember a phone
number, help you sort your socks, and invent new devices. Your brain is your idea factory.

This chapter isn't exactly about the brain itself. It is about how you can help your brain be creative by organizing your thinking. That is, the techniques in this chapter can help your idea factory produce inventive ideas.

ASK QUESTIONS

Questions are a great way to get the wheels turning in your brain. Questions help you focus on what you really need to know and understand. They help you understand the problem and see it from different perspectives. You can ask serious questions or silly ones. Both can help you find new ideas.

What questions should you ask? Six good questions to start with always are Who? What? Where? When? Why? and How? Ask these questions to help you understand what the problem is. For example, if you wanted to improve the lights used on bikes, you could start by asking the six questions. Who would use the improved light? Would kids use it or the general public or bike racers? Would it have a different design for each group? What is the

problem you are trying to solve? Is it to make a better bike light, or is it to make it easier for the rider to see the road, or is it to make it easier for other people to see the rider? Is there a solution to the problem that could be better than a bike light? Where would your invention be used? Where would you mount it on the bike? When would you turn it on and how would you do it? How would it be powered, by batteries, a generator, or something else? Why is this improvement needed?

Here's another trick: Ask how the problem would appear to other people, or how it would appear from other places.

• How would a surgeon see your problem? or a plumber?

• How would it look if you were standing on the moon? or under the sea?

• How would it look if you were standing on the inside of a machine, instead of the outside?

Analogies are another great way to get ideas. You might ask, How is the problem like eating a candy bar? How is it like cutting your lawn? How is it like going to the movies? Compare it to any unrelated activity you can imagine. It may sound crazy—your problem probably isn't very much like *any* of these things. However, by forcing your brain to make the comparison, you might get some surprising new ideas.

LOOK FOR PATTERNS

Will the solution to a different problem work with your current problem? Often inventors are successful when they take solutions from one field and apply them to problems in another. Can you see similarities between different problems?

Suppose your problem was to invent a better way to keep pizza warm during delivery. You might look to see how people have kept other foods warm—or even cold. Or, you might

23

think about ways people keep other things warm—new plants, baby chicks, their fingers and toes and ears. What patterns do you see? These other solutions may or may not work for you, but they will certainly give you ideas to try.

HAVE A BRAINSTORM

You've probably done brainstorming—a technique in which you try to get as many ideas as you can. From the very large number of ideas you generate, you are likely to find at least a few *very* good ideas.

Brainstorming can be done by one person alone, but it is more effective with a group. Each person in a group brings a different perspective and background to the problem. As they shout out their ideas, they will give everyone else new ideas. The team brainstorming together will be much more effective than all of the team members would be individually.

How do you get a large number of ideas? You do four things. First, you don't criticize *any* of the ideas as you come up with them. If you criticize them, you slow the idea process and inhibit other ideas. Think about it—wouldn't you be less willing to suggest a new idea if your last one was booed? Of course you would. So hold off any thoughts or comments on how good or bad an idea is until later. Just generate lots of them.

Second, record *all* the ideas—even the ones that sound dumb. The list can help generate new ideas later on. Each new idea can be a springboard to another idea. Another way of saying this is that you can "piggyback" one idea on another. That's why it's important to listen to everyone's ideas and record them.

Third, push yourself. Don't give up when you start to run out of ideas. Some of the best ideas come near the very end of a brainstorming session. Even when you think you've run out of ideas, keep going.

Fourth, whenever you are brainstorming, be sure to focus on the solution, not the problem. Don't say, "My problem is. . . ." Instead, say, "How can I do. . . ?" By focusing on solving the problem, you think about what you can do instead of merely what the problem is. For example, if you wanted to devise a way to keep pizza warm when you are bringing it home to eat, don't focus on "My problem is to make a pizza carrier." Instead, ask the question about how you might solve the problem, "How can I keep a pizza warm?" Since you know how to keep other things warm, you might get some ideas on how to keep a pizza warm.

After you have gobs of ideas, you need to pick a few of the best ones to work on. You need to decide in advance how you will evaluate the ideas. In other words, what makes an idea "the best"? Will the *cheapest* solution be the best one? Will the *easiest* solution be the best? Pick your criteria to select which ideas you will pursue.

SCAMPER

When you are stuck on a problem, one way to get unstuck is to think about changes you could make. The word SCAMPER can help.

SUMMER SALES SLUMP

Here's a brainstorming challenge for you and your friends to try. Say you are in the greeting card business. Business is good for Valentine's Day, Mother's Day, and even Halloween. But in August, card sales are down. Can you invent a new national holiday or remembrance day in August so you can make and sell greeting cards then? See how many ideas your team can come up with. Then pick the best five.

If you have some great ideas, maybe you should try to get a new "day" established. How would you do that? Who could help you? Start by brainstorming to get good ideas.

SCAMPER is a mnemonic device that Bob Eberle made up, based on the ideas of Alex Osborn.* The word is a way to remember a bunch of different changes you could make to start your ideas flowing again. Each letter represents one or several words that define a different sort of change.

S   Substitute

C   Combine

A   Adapt

M   Modify, Magnify, or Minify (make it bigger or smaller)

P   Put to other uses

E   Eliminate

R   Reverse or Rearrange

Here's how it works. Suppose your problem is how to keep your lunch cold until lunch time. Running through the letters of SCAMPER, you might ask:

• Can I *substitute* for materials my lunch bag is made of? Are there better insulating materials I could use?

• Can I *combine* insulators? Is there something I could wrap around the lunch bag to keep it colder?

* Bob Eberle, *SCAMPER: Games for Imagination Development* (Buffalo, N.Y.: DOK Publishers, 1971); adapted from A. F. Osborn, *Applied Imagination* (New York: Charles Scribner's Sons, 1963).

- Can I *adapt* an idea from somewhere else? What other products use insulation? Can I copy from one of these?

- Could I *modify* the lunch bag—say, into a mini-cooler?

- What *other uses* could I make of a colder lunch bag? Maybe it could keep freshly-caught fish cool on the way back to camp. Does that give me any new ideas?

- Is there anything I can *eliminate* that might be transferring heat to the inside of the box?

- Could I *rearrange* anything? For example, could I make different arrangements for how or when my lunch gets made and gets to me at school?

When you are stuck for a creative solution, remember SCAMPER. Write the word, and ask a question for each letter.

LIST THE ATTRIBUTES

Sometimes problems are so big and complex that it is hard to get started on any creative ideas. For example, suppose that you and your friends want to invent a new game. Where do you start? By listing the *attributes* of games, you will get lots of different ideas.

CONSIDER THE HUMBLE RAKE

Try a SCAMPER drill with your friends or by yourself. Take this problem: Rakes have been around for a long time, and many different types have been invented. Can you invent a better rake? Is there a better way to collect the leaves from a lawn than raking them? Can you invent a better way? See how many ideas you can come up with. Then select one or two and give them a try. You may have invented the newest gardening tool.

For example: What are the attributes of a game? Well, it might have:

a board

pieces to move

something to throw or catch

a way to keep score

good or bad luck cards

a pair of dice or a spinner

a box to keep it in

Maybe you can think of more.

Now, think about the attributes of the game's players:

who will play the game—adults, people your age, very young children

what they will wear as they play

what time of year or time of day they will play

how long they will want to play

where they will play

will they be competing or cooperating with each other

If you then tackle each of these attributes as a single problem to solve or a question to answer, you can come up with hundreds of ideas for a very creative game.

Of course, after you come up with the ideas, you'll have to evaluate them. Likely you'll throw lots of them away. Some will be too difficult to make or use. Some might be dangerous. Some will be just too goofy. But even after you throw away 90 percent of the ideas, you will be left with some really good ideas that you didn't have before.

DRAW A PICTURE

Often you can visualize a problem or its solution better than you can describe it in words. Drawing helps to unlock your creative abilities, so take pencil in hand to start thinking.

Drawing is especially good if you have some ideas of what you want, but you can't describe it very well. For example, if you wanted to design a board game, you might draw some pictures of what you think it would look like. After you have a picture, look at each piece in it. You can design each component piece from your first picture.

You can get other people's ideas by having them draw pictures for you, too. For example, you could ask people to draw the best game they could think of. Then ask them to tell what is in their drawing. Write down what they say and keep the drawings to help you remember their ideas.

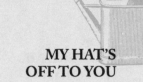

MY HAT'S OFF TO YOU

Try this challenge. Invent a new cap or hat. First, think of all the attributes of a hat, write them down. Second, think of who will wear your new cap, and when and where they will wear it. Then get creative and have fun as you think of new sizes, shapes, colors, and materials for each attribute that will appeal to the people who will wear it.

29

PICTURE ME A STORY

A creativity warm-up exercise that's lots of fun is to draw a story. Take a piece of paper and start drawing a picture. As you draw, tell a story that goes with the picture. Draw your story for friends. Then have them draw some for you.

Try a cooperative story—take turns with a friend adding something to a single picture and story.

Do any of your ideas suggest a new game?

KEEP MOVING

Don't just sit there. When you move, you *double* the number of brain cells that are active. So get up and get your brain going, too.

To get really creative, bend and move your body into the shape of whatever you are working on. Suppose you are working on how to improve a yo-yo. First stand and pretend you are using one. Then pretend you *are* a yo-yo.

Add some music and move with it. Lots of people are more creative when they are listening to music. Try this to see if it helps you. Try different types of music. Maybe country and western works for you, or maybe rock and roll, or classical, or jazz. If you can find one type that helps you create, you have a great tool to use.

KEEP AN IDEA FILE

Every day you are bombarded with new ideas you read and hear. Some of them could be useful to you when you need to solve a problem. How can you best take advantage of other people's ideas?

You create an idea file. Choose a place where you can store ideas. A file folder or a large envelope will do for starters. Then be on the lookout for great ideas.

Where do you look? Ideas are printed in your newspaper every day. Most of them are printed not on the front page (that's reserved for news or facts), but on the editorial pages and in the comics. These are great places to mine for ideas.

Another place to look for ideas is in advertisements. Advertising people make a living coming up with creative ways to get you to pay attention to products. If they succeed in getting your attention, they have a good approach. Tear successful ads out of magazines and newspapers, and file them.

When you hear a terrific idea, write it down and add it to your file. You will be surprised how often you can mine ideas from your file.

HAVE FUN

Sometimes when you get stuck on a hard problem, you get frustrated and angry. That usually doesn't help. Lighten up. Make jokes. People are more creative when they joke about the problem than when they are somber or sad.

Of course, sometimes you and your creative team can get carried away with the jokes and lose your focus on the problem. When this happens, bring everyone back to the problem, but keep the fun going.

EVALUATE YOUR IDEAS

After your brain has generated lots and lots of good ideas, remember that you have to evaluate them in order to pick some to try. With good brainstorming, you can come up with many more ideas than you have time to build. You need to pick only the best ideas for further work.

How do you evaluate ideas? You need to compare each one to a set of criteria. The criteria are the things that you think are important in a good solution. You might include how expensive the solution is, how easy it would be to make it, how much fun it would be, or how easy it would be to carry somewhere. After you have come up with your ideas for solutions, you need to write a list of the criteria you think are important.

Wherever possible, you want to find criteria that let you *measure* each solution. For example, you might be able to estimate the size of a game to see if it could fit inside your pocket or inside your car. If one of your criteria was that the game should be played in a car, it had better fit inside one. By making the criteria something you can measure, you remove the guesswork. Saying the game can't be too big doesn't tell you much. But saying it has to fit into a car gives you the chance to measure a car door and size the game to fit inside. A number is often more helpful than a general statement.

Much more difficult to determine are things like how much fun a game would be. The best way to determine this would be to ask five people which game, from your list of ideas, they would most like to play.

When you have a few ideas you think are really good, you are ready to build and test a prototype of your invention—a process that is outlined in a later chapter.

But first, there is another way of being inventive that will really appeal to you: inventing backwards. That's the subject of our next chapter.

INVENTING BACKWARDS

If you are mechanically minded, you can get great new ideas by "inventing backwards." Engineers call it "reverse engineering." You could call it "take-it-apart-for-fun." Inventing backwards, or reverse engineering, is taking apart other people's inventions to see how they work. Not only do you see how stuff works, you also get to keep all the parts. Maybe you can use them later in your own inventions.

FIVE RED-LETTER RULES

Before you start taking things apart, you need to know the rules of inventing backwards. These are extremely important, so pay attention.

Rule 1

It is considered bad form to stick a screwdriver through your hand. So, the first rule is to watch how you are using tools, especially those with sharp points. Don't point them at your hand or face, or at anyone else.

Rule 2

Inventions have springs and other components that can fly out and bite you. So, always wear glasses or lab goggles when you are taking something apart. You can buy goggles from a laboratory supply company; ask your science teacher where to get them. They are an inexpensive investment for protecting your eyes.

Rule 3

Be extra careful when taking apart electrical objects. Always take electrical plugs out of the wall sockets so that no electricity can flow into the thing you are taking apart. After you unplug it, cut off the plug and throw it away. This way no one else can plug it back in.

Some electronic devices store electrical charges in capacitors. These components can shock you. Have a knowledgeable adult check for capacitors and discharge them before you start to take apart electronic components. For safety, do not take apart television sets.

Rule 4

This is sometimes known as the law of entropy: It's easier to take something apart than to put it back together. Face it, that old camera of your mother's, laid out on the floor in hundreds of tiny pieces, is never going to take a picture again. Don't take apart anything unless you don't need it, or the owner has given you clear permission to destroy it.

Rule 5

Forget about hammers. Although hammers are useful tools, they do not belong in your toolbox when you are taking something apart. If "it" won't come loose, there is something still holding it. A hammer will only smash the whole thing. Use your eyes to find the problem instead.

WHAT'S THAT? AND THIS? AND THOSE?

Part of the process of inventing backwards is asking questions. Remember, inventors always ask lots of questions. Even before you pick up the screwdriver to take the cover off, ask yourself what you think you will find on the inside. What does this machine do? Will you find moving parts? If so, where will you find the motor? How does the motor drive the moving parts?

As you take things out, ask yourself what each part is and what it does in the machine. If you don't know what some part is, ask someone who can tell you. You might keep all the similar parts together. That way you can see how many of each type there are, and see all the different forms of each type.

Also ask yourself how you might use each part. Things like springs, gears, and knobs can be used in a variety of inventions. Circuit boards probably cannot be used, so you could throw these away.

WHERE TO FIND STUFF TO TAKE APART

Where do you get stuff to take apart? You can ask at home and around your neighborhood. Ask for things like old clocks, record players, pop-up toasters, and other objects that have moving parts. When someone offers you something good, remember Rule 4— explain clearly that you will be taking it apart and will *not* bring it back to them.

There are other places to look for stuff. Goodwill Industries and the Salvation Army collect lots of used appliances that they cannot fix. They throw these away. Ask the warehouse superintendent or manager to save a box of stuff for you.

Also, if you know someone who works at an appliance store, you could ask them to save anything they throw away.

FIXING IT UP

After you have had plenty of experience at taking things apart and recognizing what's inside, you might try to repair broken appliances. Make sure an adult checks your work if you are repairing anything that uses 110 volt, or household, electricity.

Look for the simple things you can fix, because that is where the problems are likely to be. Look for a connection that is loose, or a switch that doesn't work. Quite often the problem is caused by dirt getting inside a part, or wires coming loose.

There are several good books that can show you how to fix appliances. David Macaulay's book, *The Way Things Work,* is a good reference on machines, tools, and appliances.

Remember not to get in over your head or to promise to fix something you haven't ever taken apart. Fixing isn't inventing, but it's fun, and it can give you good ideas for inventing.

Inventing backwards isn't to everyone's taste, but *everyone* can enjoy inventing forwards. The next chapter will help you get started.

LUCKY CHARLES

Many great inventors learned about machinery by taking things apart. One of these was Charles Kettering, the inventor of the first electrical ignition system and self starter for cars. He also invented the first practical engine-driven generator, as well as safety glass and Freon. When Kettering was a boy, he took apart his mother's new sewing machine. His parents thought that he had destroyed the expensive machine. They were ready to punish him. But then he confidently put it back together again. And it worked. Don't press your luck, though. Before you try taking apart something valuable, get lots of experience on discarded appliances. And make sure you have permission of the owner. You may not be as skilled or as lucky as Charles Kettering was.

INVENT BY SOLVING PROBLEMS

"Build a better mousetrap and the world will beat a path to your doorstep," the old saying goes. But actually, catching mice isn't such a big business these days, and well over 1,000 devices have already been invented to catch mice. So the world may not jump for joy if you invent one more mousetrap.

But the idea is right. If you can solve a problem easier, better, or cheaper with your invention, the world may take notice. This is true especially if the problem you solved was a common one, with many people wishing for an easier, better, or cheaper solution.

By now you know what an inventor is, and that you are one. You know how to come up with creative solutions to problems through brainstorming and other methods. And you know how to invent backwards.

Now it's time to invent forward. Let's look for a problem to solve.

WE ALL HAVE PROBLEMS

Everyone has problems—the rich, the poor, and everyone in between. You have problems. Some of them may be solvable with an invention. Let's look in your life for such a problem.

How does your day start? When you wake up, is there anything that annoys you? Is there something that gets your day off to a bad start? Is the light in your bedroom too bright when you first turn it on? Is the bathroom floor cold on your feet? Are your shoes scrambled in the mess on the floor? Does the breakfast cereal spill when you try to pour it into a bowl?

As you get ready for school, does everything fit neatly into your book bag? At school, will you be able to find quickly what you need in the bag? While you are waiting for the bus, does your neck get cold or your hair get wet in the rain?

You get the idea. If you pay attention to all the little annoyances in your day, you will find lots of problems to solve. If you have a problem, other people probably have the same problem. By solving *your* problem, you may also solve a problem for many other people.

Your friends have problems, too. Ask them what their problems are. Do several people have similar problems? If they do, you may have a problem worth solving.

THE ANNOYING BOOK BAG

Let's say you talk to your friends and everyone agrees that their bookbags are less than perfect. "Not big enough." "Rips too easily." "No way to organize the stuff inside." "No one uses the shoulder straps." Here you have some great problems to solve.

Stop here for a moment to consider the potential. How many kids use bookbags? They're used not just in high school and junior high, but also in elementary school, and even in college. You could ask the information desk at your library to look up the number, but let's just say it's a zillion.

That's a lot. If you could sell one bag to each student each year, and if you netted $1 for each sale, you'd be a zillionaire. Maybe you wouldn't sell quite that many. Still, you know

DOLLAR SIGNS
IN YOUR EYES

How big is the market for a new,
improved bookbag? If there were one
zillion students who might buy your
bag, only a small number actually will.
Many will stay with their old bags.
Some won't like your styling. Some
won't think your improvements are
important. Some will buy cheaper bags.
Maybe if you work hard and are lucky,
you could capture 10 percent of the total
market. That would be quite an
accomplishment in a field that is
crowded with companies already
making bookbags. Maybe a more
realistic number would be 1 percent. Of
course, 1 percent of a zillion is still a lot
of sales. If it is enough to warrant the
expense of developing the bag, setting
up the manufacturing plant, setting up

that a very large number of students carry bookbags. And you know that they buy new ones every year or two. So the potential sales for an improved bookbag are large.

But don't start spending that money yet. First you need a product that solves the problems everyone mentioned.

A NEW, IMPROVED BOOKBAG

How do you invent a new bag? You start by doing some creative thinking. You could do some brainstorming with some friends or by yourself. Write out the problems with existing bags, and ask what features on a new bag would eliminate or reduce these problems. See how many different solutions you can come up with for each problem.

Some of your solutions may not work at all. After you brainstorm, do some critical thinking to decide which solutions seem best.

You might decide that you can't solve *all* the problems your friends mentioned. Some people might have said their bag was too small, and someone else might have said it was too large. You won't be able to please everyone, so concentrate on the problems that seem most important and on solutions that seem doable.

While you are working on your ideas, keep notes. This is important. Get a notebook, preferably one that is bound just like a hardback book, but with blank pages that you should number. Keep your ideas here. Draw your designs here. This is your inventor's log, and it can be used in patent cases in court. So make your written work neat and accurate. Show your notebook to someone periodically. Ask them to sign and date the pages. This will show when you came up with each idea.

After drawing some plans in your notebook, it's time to try your ideas in a *mock-up* of a new, improved bookbag. You might start with an old bag and make changes to it. Your mock-up doesn't need to look like a store-bought bookbag. At this point, work quickly and skip the details.

Try the mock-up. Carry it around with books and things in it. See what works and what doesn't. Quickly change what doesn't work, and try it again. There is no sense investing lots of time in the mock-up of a new feature that may not work. Work quickly so you can make lots of adjustments.

When you have a mock-up that really works well, make a *prototype.* This is where you will invest the most time. Your prototype should look and feel the same as the finished product will.

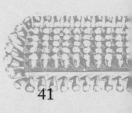

marketing and distribution networks, and doing all the accounting, you can start a company. Not easy, but it happens everyday in America. Of course, you don't have to do all that work yourself. You could sell your design to a company that is already in the bookbag business. They have the factories, the salespeople, and the ability to buy needed materials at discounts you couldn't approach. To sell your idea to a company, you need to have a good estimate of how big the potential market is, and be able to convince people how wonderful your idea is.

With your prototype—which might be one, two, or three bags—you can test the market. Give your new bookbags to some friends who have agreed to test them for you. As part of the agreement, they can use the new bags for a few days. In return, they will give you an evaluation of the new model. You might give them a list of questions to answer, so they will think about the things that most concern you.

After your friends have tried the bags, get them together in a group to discuss what they liked and didn't like. Fair warning: This may be the hardest part of inventing for you. When your friends describe something they didn't like, don't get angry and try to defend it. Don't argue with them. Listen and take notes. If two or more people agree on what is right or wrong, accept their advice.

When you have completed the market test, make any needed adjustments and changes. Actually, you may go through this stage several times before you get your bookbag just the way you want it. With each new prototype, you can go back to your friends and ask them to try your totally new and radically improved bookbag.

When you are convinced that you have the right invention, that it has just the right combination of improvements, you are ready to take it to the market. Your "market" might be an invention contest, a class project, a real bookbag manufacturer—even retail stores, if you will make the bags yourself. You can read more about these options in "Making Your Inventions Pay Off."

SIX STEPS TO SUCCESS

Here is an outline of the steps we followed in the example of the bookbag. The same steps will work with just about any new invention.

Step 1. Find a problem

Finding problems to solve is part of a lifelong quest to discover what really bugs people. Watch people, listen to them, and take notes to put in your idea file. Once people know you are inventing solutions to problems, they will bring their problems to you

Step 2. Focus on smaller problems

Break down the big problem (bookbags) into smaller problems that you can get a handle on (for example, they're too small, the straps are awkward, they're hard to organize). Brainstorm to find solutions. You may not find good solutions for *all* the smaller problems, so decide which ones you can solve and skip the rest. Pick your best solutions and give them a try.

Step 3. Build a mock-up

The mock-up is something you should make quickly. Try it and rebuild it. Keep adding new features. While you are working on the mock-up, you may think of dozens of new solutions. The more you tinker with it, the better it will get. You may find that you are more creative when you are working with the mock-up than you were working with ideas on a piece of paper. Many people generate their best ideas when they are tinkering with their hands.

Step 4. Build a prototype

When you are happy with your mock-up, build a prototype and test it. Really listen to the feedback you get. Each person's opinions provide valuable information to help you make your invention better.

Step 5. Keep trying

After you have the comments from your testers, you may want to go back to the brainstorming phase or the mock-up phase. Remember, Edison went back 1,800 times before he got the light bulb right.

Step 6. Find your market

When you are convinced that your invention is as good as you can make it, go to market. What this could mean for you is discussed further in the last chapter, "Making Your Inventions Pay Off."

HOW TO FIND PROBLEMS

Here are some methods that will help you generate lists of problems you could work on. On pages 45–46, there's a list of 30 problems to give you the idea. However, you really need to make your *own* list. That way you'll find problems you really care about.

When you're in an inventing mood, you can mine your list for ideas. Not every problem will have a solution that requires an invention. But some will. Keep the list and review it now and then. Each time you look at it, you may come up with another invention idea.

To make your own list, you might start by listing things that annoy you. What is most annoying at home? at school? in the kitchen? at the mall? in the car? at movie theaters? in front of the television? while brushing your teeth? Add to your list whenever you think of something that bothers you.

Another way to create your personal list of problems is to start by listing all the things you like to do. What sporting activities do you like? Do you enjoy reading? being with friends? listening to music? baking things? drawing cartoons? shopping? List everything you like to do with your time. Once you have this list, write down the chief problems or annoyances you run into during each activity.

Here's a third way to make a problem list: Start by listing all the tools you use in your daily life. Your list may include pens, pencils, scissors, sewing needles, hammers, wrenches, computers, spoons, mixing bowls, rakes, brooms. Then, think of the difficulties of using each of them. If you can solve one problem of a common tool, you will have a useful invention.

People do this all the time. Someone invented the Veg-O-Matic to slice and dice better than ordinary knives. People invent new types of wrenches, even though there are hundreds of kinds of wrenches already. Even a small improvement can be a great-selling invention.

WHAT THIS COUNTRY NEEDS

Use the following list as a starting point, as a tool to get your creative juices flowing.

What this country needs is . . .

1. a better bookbag
2. a better lunchbox
3. a way to keep pizza warm on the way home from the pizzeria
4. a better way to lock your bike
5. a bandage you can put on with one hand
6. a return device to go on a basketball hoop so the ball come back to you
7. a resealable lid for soft drink cans
8. a device that feeds birds or pets

9. a way to record phone messages so you can read them

10. a better device to clean venetian blinds

11. a new educational game

12. a puzzle about ecology

13. a storage container for videotapes or game cartridges

14. a faster, more controllable sled

15. a bike light that works

16. a better mosquito repellent

17. sound insulation you can put on walls to deaden the sound of someone's stereo

18. a lock for a house that doesn't require a key

19. a room alarm to scare off your younger brother or sister

20. a sunburn alarm

21. a device to store and bundle newspapers

22. a good way to keep track of friends' phone numbers

23. a device to clean up pets' messes

24. fog-proof mirrors for bathrooms

25. a ketchup bottle lid that doesn't get messy

26. a device to help you hit a nail with a hammer

27. a self-cleaning spoon for messy pet food

28. a doormat that stays in place while it cleans your shoes

29. a bike kickstand that always holds up your bike

30. a book end that doesn't fall over or slide

CHOOSING WHICH PROBLEMS TO SOLVE

After you have a good list of problems, you need to focus on one or a few. You can pick any problems you want. Here are some criteria for picking a good problem:

- It has to be fun. If it is drudgery, you won't keep at it. To be successful in inventing, you must be persistent. You won't be persistent if you don't like what you are doing.

- It has to be a problem you can solve. Don't pick "inventing a fusion nuclear reactor" unless you have the prerequisite skills or are willing to take the time to learn them. Of course, you don't have to have *every* skill—welding, plumbing, sewing—that will be needed to make the product. You can hire other people with these skills to do the work, or "job it out" to businesses that do the work. However, an inventor cannot job out the creative thinking and project management. That's why you really do need to know a lot about what you are inventing.

- It should be a problem many people share. If you want to sell your idea, someone has to buy it. They will buy it *if* they share the same problem, and *if* your invention solves it for them better than the other solutions that are available.

THE IDEA NO ONE WANTED

Thomas Edison's first patent was for an electrical vote recorder. After he had invented it, he found that no one wanted to buy it. At that point he vowed never again to expend his time inventing something unless he was sure that someone would buy it.

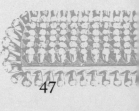

47

Of course, you can invent just for the fun of it, or to solve problems that only you have. That's fine, too. But if you want to sell your invention, make sure someone wants it before you go to the trouble of doing the inventing. You may have other personal criteria to consider when picking a problem to solve. For example, if you sew well, you may want to concentrate on projects that involve sewing. Also think about the time, the workspace, and the tools you have available. As you practice inventing, you'll develop a better sense of the type of problems you enjoy working on.

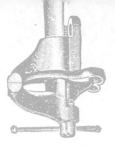

INVENT BY FINDING NEW USES FOR THINGS

In "Invent by Solving Problems," you saw how to invent something by starting with a problem and seeking an invention to solve it. That's the way most people expect inventions to occur. But there are other ways. Many inventions are really solutions looking for problems. You may have the invention, but not know what to do with it. Is that hard to believe? The laser is one example.

THE TOOL WITH A HUNDRED USES

People worked for years to develop the concepts of the laser and to make the first working models. But once lasers became a reality, many people asked what good they were. Lasers seemed to be an interesting oddity with little value.

However inventors have since found hundreds of uses for lasers. They are used in agriculture and in construction to make sure a field or house is level. In medicine, surgeons use the heating action of lasers to destroy damaged tissue. In industry, lasers are used for cutting materials, welding, and making tiny holes in materials. Lasers are used extensively to

measure the distances in surveying and scientific research. You see laser machinery when you buy something at a grocery store using optical scan price codes, or when you use a laser printer with a computer. Today, it seems we couldn't do without lasers.

A SECOND LOOK

Just as in the case of lasers, you might have better luck starting with an "invention" and searching for new problems it could solve. Think of all the inventions that we often use just once, for one specific job, and then throw away. Here are some common one-use items:

camera film canisters

auto tires

empty frozen juice cans

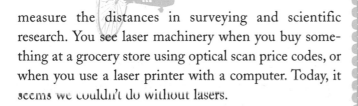

tin cans

plastic bags

plastic milk jugs

paper towel tubes

egg cartons

worn out tennis balls

newspapers

paper bags

magazines

plastic rings that hold six-packs

NEW HOME FOR THE FISH?

For years, people worked to design artificial ocean reefs using worn tires. The idea seemed great. The reefs would provide new habitat for fish and other marine life, and millions of used tires are taking up valuable space in landfills. Using tires for reefs seemed to remedy two problems. Unfortunately, this solution didn't work. It turns out that it is easier and more efficient to make reefs by dumping used concrete from old bridges and roads than it is to make reefs out of tires. But this is the type of problem hunting that can come up with new inventions.

WHO THOUGHT
OF IT FIRST?

The laser provides an interesting example of how confusing the patent system can be. The laser was conceived independently by Charles Townes and Gordon Gould. Ted Maiman made the first working laser. All three inventors hold patents on the laser. Each could be (and is) called the father of the laser. For many years, laser manufacturers paid royalties to Townes as the rightful inventor and patent holder of the laser.

Townes had invented the maser *(microwave amplification by stimulated emission of radiation) and later applied for the first patent on* lasers *(light amplification by stimulated emission of radiation). Gould was a graduate student studying under Townes.*

Some of these can be recycled and have value as a resource. But for the most part, these materials are both unwanted and in large supply. Take a second look. How else might they be used? If you can find another use for any of these, you could have a great invention.

New technology is another place to look for solutions in need of problems. New inventions are being introduced every day. Some magazines such as *Popular Science* or *Popular Mechanics* carry listings of new products in their field. If you can see another use for the new technology, you could have a winner.

For example, a new motion detector, developed as a burglar alarm, may have many other uses. Could you use it to make a baby crib alarm? When a sleeping baby wakes up and starts to move, that could trigger a signal to alert the parents. Or, the motion detector could turn on soothing music to put baby back to sleep.

Just as new technology offers many opportunities for inventing, so does *old* technology. In some fields, the pace of technology is very rapid, and businesses are replacing equipment every few year. As newer and faster computers come on the market, the old ones are cast aside. In most cases, no one wants them. The same holds true for typewriters, copiers, printers, and computer modems. Take a second look at the discards. Can you come up with new uses for them? Can you come up with uses for some of their parts?

Look around you for other solutions that need problems. Too often, we look at things and see only what they are, not what they could be.

He developed the idea for the laser, and coined the word laser, *but didn't seek a patent.*

He thought he didn't have to apply for the patent then. Years later, he did apply for a patent, using his inventor's log as his evidence. After many expensive legal battles, Gould won and became wealthy from the patent royalties.

Maiman developed the first operational laser in 1960. Many other types of lasers have been developed since then.

53

PROJECTS FOR CREATIVE TINKERING

Do you know how to tinker? When you tinker with something, you fiddle around with it, trying different things to see what it will do, or how you can make it do something different. You may have a goal in mind, or you might just be fooling around. This experimental play can lead to ideas on how to use or improve an invention. Play can be productive as well as fun.

While your hands are busy tinkering, leave your mind open to new discoveries. Some people could look at a new opportunity for hours and never really see it because they weren't prepared for it. The more prepared your mind is, the more likely you are to see possibilities and take advantage of what your hands discover.

Being prepared means soaking up knowledge on as many subjects as you can. It also means asking yourself questions. What could I use this for? What other uses are there for this? How could I change this to make something better? By asking questions, you prepare your mind for new opportunities.

Many of the ideas that emerge from playing around will apply quite naturally to games, puzzles, and toys. This could be a great place to concentrate your inventive efforts. Having played games for years, you are an expert on what makes a good game. You and your friends know what is new, what is good, and what is terrible in the toy and game market.

You probably have the equivalent of a Ph.D. in messing around with games, puzzles, and toys. This expertise can be useful.

You don't have to concentrate solely on the toy market. However, it is a good place to start. You can let other ideas grow out of your tinkering with notions for toys.

This chapter suggests three types of projects for you to tinker with: Move-It projects, Make-It projects, and Zap-It projects. Pick a project from any one of these categories to get started. Work on one until you meet a technical problem you cannot solve, or until it isn't fun any more. Then start on a different one.

Working on several different problems at one time can be good. You may even find that working on one project helps you solve problems in another. Also, the longer you work on a project, the more good ideas you will have. So don't give up altogether when you get stuck on a project. Instead, put it aside for a while and work on something else. Later, you can go back to the stalled project. Maybe, after this rest, you will find new energy and ideas to complete it.

As you get good ideas, write them down in your inventor's log. You can look back at your log later and maybe find an idea you need. A glance at your log could jog your memory, bringing together a problem and its solution.

MOVE-IT PROJECTS

Think of all the energy used in moving people and materials from one place to another. Think of all the different machines we have to do this. And think how many games and toys involve movement.

Inventors have spent lifetimes working on improving transportation systems—from cars to rocket ships, from elevators to helicopters, and from catapults to trains. Yet there are

FOR FUN AND PROFIT

Toys, games, and puzzles can make a lot of money for their inventors. According to Inside Santa's Workshop, *a book by Richard Levy and Ronald Weingartner, Americans spend more than $13 billion a year on toys. Consider that more than 200 million people around the world have played with one type of toy, Lego building blocks. Matchbox Toys (USA) out produces all other makers of vehicles in the world. They make about 100 million toy cars and trucks each year. The game Monopoly has sold over 100 million copies. That's not bad for a game that the experts expected to be a fad ending in the late 1930s. There are three times the number of G. I. Joe and Barbie dolls combined as there are people in this country. Toys are big business.*

still lots of opportunities left for you to do some inventing. Whether you feel like sliding, pushing, floating, flying, rolling, squirting, spinning, or tossing, here are some projects to get you started.

Slide it

Make an air hockey table. Provide air from the exhaust or blowing side of a heavy-duty shop vacuum or other vacuum cleaner. Figure out the size and spacing of the air holes and the surface you want to use. A cardboard box will do. If you want to use a wooden surface, attach plastic sheeting around the base of the wood and run the vacuum exhaust into the bag. What games could you make using this?

Invent a better sled. Some sleds have runners. Others have a curved bottom surface. Can you make one that goes faster, is more steerable, or is just better looking? If you live in a warm climate, can you make a sled to slide down grassy hills or sand dunes?

Make a slider. If you had something that slid across a surface really easily, you could use it in all sorts of games. How could you make such a slider? Can you find metal ball bearings to use? If not, try substituting golf balls. Figure out how to hold them together so they slide as one unit.

Invent a Hovercraft. If you were to turn over a large air hockey table, could you make a Hovercraft? Consider using a half sheet of ¾-inch plywood, cut into a circle. Attach a piece of heavy plastic sheeting to the sides. Cut only a few holes, each two to three inches in diameter, in the plastic. Connect the center of the plastic sheeting to the bottom on the plywood so it forms a donut shape when filled with air. Use the exhaust from your vacuum to pump in air. Your Hovercraft will glide most easily over smooth, polished floors, because it is not really a Hovercraft, but a "Hoover"-craft—or a vacuum-powered slider.

You can make a small model Hovercraft with a plastic lid, the squirt nozzle from a liquid detergent bottle, and a balloon. The blown-up balloon provides air to the underside, or table side, of the lid. The nozzle, glued to the lid, lets you attach the balloon to the Hovercraft. The air from the balloon flows through the nozzle and through a hole in the lid to lift it off the floor. Can you get one of these models to slide down a ramp? Will it travel over water?

Push it

Build a car. It could be big enough for you to ride in, or it could be a small model. For large cars, you will need heavy materials and solid wheels. You could use wheels from a lawn mower, an outdoor grill, a bicycle, a wheelbarrow, or a skateboard. You could even cut them from wood. In general, the larger the wheel is, the better it will roll. How will you steer this vehicle? With your feet? With your hands? Will the front wheels steer, or the back wheels? How many wheels will you have? What is the frame made of? Will you power it—say, with a lawn mower engine? Or will you power it with gravity and use it for downhill races?

A model car is easier to work on since it doesn't have to carry your weight and doesn't need the safety features that you would want in a vehicle that carries people. A model car could be powered with gravity (downhill), rubber bands (twisted or stretched), balloons, a sail, or a spring (like a mousetrap). You might even figure a way to jet propel it, using a simple chemical reaction (like the one that results when you mix baking soda and vinegar). The body might be made of wood (like the Boy Scouts' Pinewood Derby cars), or plastic, or might be a combination of parts from a construction kit or model kit.

Make a hand truck or dolly. A hand truck is a two-wheeled, rolling lever to lift heavy objects and roll them where you want them. Here is something you and your family could use around home. Can you make a two- or four-wheeled cart to carry the garbage cans to the street, or to help move furniture?

Design a monorail. With some string and a wheel or two, you could develop a monorail system to send messages or small packages back and forth. Or, you could use a string and a straw, guiding a balloon, to make a monorail. Tape the balloon to the straw that is threaded onto the string. If the string is held taut, a filled balloon can propel itself 50 feet down the string.

With a heavy line and pulley, you could make a trolley slide to carry you and friends across your yard. Have a knowledgeable adult check out your system before you try a death-defying ride.

Float it

Build a boat. Model boats can be made from a wide variety of materials. You could use discarded food containers, fruits or vegetables, or modeling clay, as well as more traditional materials such as wood. Power for your boat could come from rubber bands, sails (and fans), balloons, or the small battery-powered electric motors used in models.

Warning: For anything that goes in the water, use only the motors that take batteries. Do not use electric motors that need to be plugged into a wall outlet.

If you can make a boat, can you invent a submarine? This is a more difficult problem, because you need to get the buoyancy adjusted so your craft will float below the water surface.

Develop a parachute. There are lots of games you could try with parachutes. Can you drop an egg 10 feet and have it enjoy a safe landing by using a parachute? Simple parachutes can be made from plastic bags. Can you find a better design? How about one that works like an airplane wing so it doesn't go straight down, but glides down?

Use balloon power. Balloons can be used in many different ways. Helium-filled balloons can give you lift to float things. Air-filled balloons can provide power to move things. Try attaching a straw to the end of a filled balloon and letting it go. Can you add wings to it?

Fly it

Fly a kite. Nearly everyone likes to fly a kite. Can you invent a new or better kite? Can you make up kite games to go with your kite? How about a kite story?

Make an airplane. You might start with some model paper airplanes. There are books that describe a wide variety of models to build. For example, you can find some unusual ideas in a book by Stephen Weiss, *Wings and Things: Origami That Flies.* Maybe you can create your own new style. Once you have several planes, how could you use them? Can you make up a game or contest using paper airplanes?

If you like model airplanes, consider making a wind tunnel to test them in. Use a powerful fan and a small tunnel (made of cardboard or wood) to see how your planes will fly. Can you use the wind tunnel to predict how your models will fly outside?

Design a rocket. There are many ways to build rockets. You can use the model kits sold at hobby stores, or you can make your own rockets. One of the simplest ways to launch a rocket is using air pressure and water.

You can launch a two-liter plastic soft-drink bottle 60 feet in the air using just a bicycle pump and a bunch of parts from a hardware store. You need to be able to hold the bottle tightly against a wooden launchpad. A piece of neoprene rubber attached to the wood will ensure that air doesn't escape from the bottle while you are pumping it up. Two metal bars can clamp against the bottle neck to hold it tightly against the neoprene.

Warning: You must secure the bottle well, because an accidental launch could surprise and hurt someone.

You can hook the bicycle pump to a tire valve stem that is clamped into a section of hose. The other end of the hose can fit into a piece of PVC tubing that fits into the bottle. Put some water into the bottle, clamp it in place, pump it up, and launch it.

Roll it

Make a raceway. Raceways are tubes or tracks that you construct for balls to roll down. You can make roller coaster rides, loop-the-loops, and other amusement rides for a golf ball or tennis ball. For tracks, consider cardboard folded into a V or U cross section, PVC or mailing tubes cut in half along their length, plastic molding, or flexible hose.

You could fix the tracks in place, or you might make them transportable. If you want to be able to transport them, you could attach the tracks to pegboard. Or, you could glue Velcro on one side of the tracks or tubes. Then you can stick them to the carpeted surface of a piece of wood or a wall. Design the most amusing arrangement of curves and noise-makers for your ball to hit as it rolls down the raceway.

Build a "Rube." Years ago, a popular newspaper cartoonist drew very elaborate, wacky, chain-reaction inventions to accomplish very simple tasks. A Rube Goldberg device might take 15 to 20 steps to catch a mouse, to turn on a toaster, or to turn out the lights. People would love to watch such devices in action. Maybe you've played the Milton Bradley game Mouse Trap, which is based on this sort of chain-reaction contraption. Can you build your own Rube Goldberg device, as a piece of sculpture and amusement?

Go bowling. Rolling balls toward targets is a popular pastime around the world. There is ten pin bowling, duck pin bowling, lawn bowling, and boccie. Can you invent a new type of bowling?

Squirt it

Pump it up. Flowing or squirting water attracts attention. People love to watch water fountains or water sculptures. You can make your own hand-operated water pumps, using materials you might find at home. Bernie Zubrowski's book, Messing Around with Water Pumps and Siphons, is a good place to look for ideas. You can also use the pumps found in the bottles of household products. Use the hand pumps—don't try to use cans that are pressurized.

Warning: Be careful to wash out any bottle thoroughly and don't use a bottle that contained a nasty substance.

In designing landscapes that have water, people typically pump water uphill and let it flow back down along some interesting or attractive background. You could make water wheels (turbines), dams, or lakes for small boats. Or you could make a natural-looking waterfall. Or you could squirt water out at various points, like a fountain.

Squirt it out. Water pistols make a great start for new games or contests. Knocking over targets is one obvious idea. What else can you come up with? Could you create a game that might be sold with water pistols? Possibly a squirt-gun manufacturer would be interested in such a game, to help boost sales of their products.

Spin it

Top this! Tops are great fun for all ages. You can make them from a variety of materials. Could you combine tops and raceways to make a downward racecourse for spinning tops?

Gyroscopes are tops. You could use one to make a boat go in a straight line. What other uses can you devise for gyroscopes?

Frisbees spin like tops. Can you make a new style of Frisbee? Start with a few paper plates and fashion them into different designs.

Design a whirlybird. With a rubber band and a small propeller, you can make a helicopter. It will take a few tries to get one to go high. Maybe you could try one with several propellers. Try carving propellers out of pieces of wood or cutting them out of cardboard. See what shape gives you the best results.

Make a "movie." You probably know that a motion picture film is really a series of still pictures. To make your eyes see moving pictures instead of a series of still images, you need to show your eye at least 10 pictures per second. One way to do this is to make a zoetrope. You can make one from a cylindrical container like a round ice-cream carton, one-gallon size or larger. You need to figure out how to make the cylinder spin, so it turns smoothly. You might support it from the ceiling with string, or put it on a turntable. Cut slots in the side of the cylinder so you can view the opposite inside wall. Then, draw 10 to 12 sequential pictures on a piece of paper that fits inside the cylinder, around its walls. You can make all sorts of moving pictures this way. For more ideas, see *The Zoetrope Book* by Roger Kukes.

Toss it

Catapult it. Catapults are fun to make. How many ways can you catapult a tennis ball? You could use rubber bands or bungee cords. You could use a spring. Or you could drop a weight on the end of a lever.

Could you devise a vacuum launcher for a small ball? Hook up a mailing tube to the exhaust side of a vacuum cleaner. Drop the ball in the tube and turn on the vacuum. Of course, this isn't a catapult—it's a "blow-it-out-the-tube" device.

Boomerang it. Can you make a boomerang that really returns to the thrower? Look at the shape of a boomerang, and try to make one yourself. Try varying the shape or adding wings to it. When you launch it, make sure you have plenty of open space so you won't hit anyone.

Just throw it. When you get right down to it, one of the most enjoyable things in life is hefting a rock or a ball and letting it fly toward a target. It's also fun to play catch with someone—even your dog. Invent a new ball, or a new way to throw a ball (maybe a launching stick?), or a new game based on a thrown ball. If people continue to play your game days after you have shown it to them, you'll know you have a winner.

Aim here. Many tossing games involve good aim. Using beanbags or balls, we sometimes try to knock over a target, or get our balls or bags into a basket. There are lots of ways to play these games. Invent your own throwing bag and target, and come up with some new rules.

You don't have to touch the ball or bag, of course. You could hit it with a golf club (miniature golf), or a tennis racket, or almost anything else. You could use rings instead of balls or bags, and aim for a stake in the ground.

MAKE-IT PROJECTS

Designing and building things is great fun. You start by being creative and coming up with a new design or recipe. Then you get your hands and mind together to make it. Then you get people to look at it, listen to it, or taste it. And then, or course, you get new ideas of how to make it better for the next time.

Build it

Putting together model buildings and bridges is great fun. It is also a good way to see how a real building or bridge will work before it is built. Here are a few ideas on constructing model structures, and what you can do with them.

Design a building. Drinking straws, paper or plastic, are a good material to use for building. They are inexpensive, lightweight, and strong. You can connect them with paper clips, masking tape, or by jamming the end of one straw into the opening of another. To use paper clips, bend the clip open into a V-shape. Put one end in one straw, the other end in the second straw.

Challenge your friends to see who can build the tallest tower under certain constraints: maybe using no more than 100 straws, or within a certain time limit, or using five inches of masking tape.

Cardboard milk cartons, if you can still get them, also make good building materials. If straws represent metal or wood framing for a building, these milk cartons can represent bricks or blocks. You will need to fold the pouring end of each carton so it will lie flat and make a brick. Fill them with sand or dirt to give your bottom bricks some weight and stability. Can you make an arch out of the bricks?

Other materials to consider are balsa wood, ice-cream sticks, toothpicks, rolled newspaper, egg crates, paper towel tubes, and soft drink cans. You will have to invent fasteners for each of these materials.

Build a bridge. Bridges are challenging structures to build. How long can you make a bridge span? How much weight can your bridge hold before it collapses? There are several different types of bridges, ranging from slabs of materials spanning a creek or ravine, to suspension bridges and truss bridges. Look at the bridge designs used in your town. Pick one design and a building material (ice-cream sticks or toothpicks and white glue work well), and try to make a model of it. Then invent your own design. Test your model bridge to see how much weight it can hold.

Protect it. Each year, millions of packages are sent back and forth across the country and around the world. How many of them get damaged? Too many, that's for sure. Can you find a better way to package delicate items?

Start by devising the packaging to protect a raw egg when dropped from two or three stories up. (Be sure that no one will pass underneath your experiment during the dropping part.) Try your packaging under different conditions—try different weights (two or three eggs); see if the package still works when it is wet.

Challenge your friends to see who can make the lightest package that protects an egg while being dropped from a tall building. Make sure the building owner gives you permission. Al Renner has some great ideas on egg-drop containers in his book, *How to Build a Better Mousetrap Car.*

Build something else. There is a world of other items you could build. You might make an ant farm . . . a new filter for your fish tank . . . a coat rack . . . a kitchen stool . . . a box to store things in. Choose some building materials and just start tinkering—you might be surprised at what you get!

Play with it

Make music. How many ways are there to make music with unmusical objects? You could create new stringed instruments, percussion instruments, and horns. Maybe you could outfit an entire unorthodox band. See if you can play a real tune on your new instrument—then test it on your friends, to see if anyone can recognize the tune. Can you make instruments out of the parts from discarded appliances? If so, you could call yourself "The Old Technology Band."

Figure it out. For every puzzle in the world, there is a person somewhere who made it up. Puzzles can be pictures cut into hundreds of small pieces—those are jigsaw puzzles. Puzzles can also be three-dimensional brain teasers—like Rubik's Cube. There are also mazes—both on paper, and three-dimensional. Look at the puzzles in a novelty store or magic shop to get some ideas of the types of things other people have come up with. Then, go invent a new one.

Design a board game. Board games are enormously popular throughout the world. From age-old games like checkers and chess, to more recent games like Monopoly and Clue, board games are played by millions of people. And each year, people invent new ones. Make up a game, maybe about your favorite hobby, or vacation place, or food. You may want to include the element of chance; this is usually provided by dice, or a spinner, or cards. Keep the game simple. Try it on your friends.

Create a playspace. Can you design and create a new playhouse or doll house for the younger children in your family? You could make a traditional house, or one from the 25th century. Maybe it could be an underwater house, or a house for living on Mars.

Just as much fun is making a play town. Start with an old blanket or sheet. From colored cloth, cut out shapes representing houses, fire stations, police stations, an airport, roads, hospitals, factories, and more. You can glue or sew these onto the sheet or blanket, making an entire play town. Add some toy cars, and you have the makings of many afternoons of fun for little people. Test out a mock-up with the children in your neighborhood.

Make a puppet. Puppets are a very old form of dramatic entertainment. Design a puppet for your own amusement. It might be a traditional form—a marionette, a shadow puppet, a hand puppet, or a finger puppet. Or maybe you can invent a new type. Design a theater for it and take your show on the road. Make a game out of operating a puppet. Can you make the puppet pick up a small object, or throw a ball?

Concoct it

Make something stretchy. You don't have to have a chemistry lab to make basic materials to use in new ways. For example, you can make rubber bands to meet your specific needs. Buy liquid latex at a hobby shop. Add vinegar to the latex to make it pliable so you can form objects of rubber.

Invent your own paper. Lots of materials, from cotton rags to vegetable clippings, can be used to make paper. Look up paper making in an encyclopedia. Vary the recipe to make your own.

Squish it. Make your own version of Silly Putty modeling clay. Start with two parts of Elmer's Glue-All and one part of liquid starch. Mix it up. You can add liquid food coloring for interest. Try different variations on this formula to see what works best.

Bake it. You can do lots of inventing in the kitchen by developing new recipes. Start with proven recipes and then vary the ingredients. Invent your own dessert, or bread, and enter it in a baking contest.

ZAP-IT PROJECTS

People have been inventing devices that use electricity for over two hundred years. And people invent new ones all the time. From computers to electrical can openers, our world runs on electricity. You can get electricity to do almost anything you want, if you are creative. When working on "Zap-It Projects," only use electricity from batteries you have in your home or school.

Electrify it

Light it up. Using a few batteries, wire, and light bulbs, what can you do? Can you make a device that will turn lights on and off in a series? With various switches, can you make a light show?

Try using a metal can for a switch. Paint the can all over, except in places where you want it to conduct electricity. As you rotate the can, the wires leading to the lights can come in contact with the bare metal to make a circuit. As the can continues to turn and the wires contact the painted surface again, the light goes off. How else can you switch lights on and off?

You can make a "quiz board" using the lights and batteries. For example, create a quiz that involves matching items on two lists. The quiz taker touches one exposed wire to an item on the first list, and the second wire to a matching item on the second list. If you wire the lights correctly, they will light up only when someone correctly matches two items. You can change the questions easily by writing them on a piece of paper that you tape into place on the quiz board.

Catch a thief. What kind of switches do you need to make a burglar alarm? Can you make some? You can buy photo diodes (for electric eyes) and magnetic switches (for door or window alarms) at an electronic supply store. While there, check out their other supplies and ideas for suggested projects. Using electronic components, you can make hundreds of devices—from alarms, to amplifiers, to fish callers.

Telegraph it. Try setting up a communications system using Morse code, or a code of your own. Can you get more than two people on your system? How far apart can you be? How proficient can you and your friends get at sending and receiving messages?

To send messages, you can use lights, or buzzers, or flags. To make a simple code, assign each letter of the alphabet to another letter or number. For example, let N in code represent A. If only you and your friends have the decoder, it will be difficult for someone else to read your messages.

Invent a code, and then see if a friend can break it. That is, can your friend decode the message without knowing the code? If someone can break your code, can you figure out a way to make it more difficult to break?

Magnetize it. Make an electromagnet. Wrap wire around a nail or a bar of iron. Connect the ends of the wire to a battery. Make sure you wrap lots of wire. How much is enough? Try picking up tacks with different numbers of coils of wire. Once you have an electromagnet, can you make an electric motor?

Tell time. Clocks are all around us. The earliest clocks used shadows from the sun, dripping water, falling sand, or burning candles. Can you make a clock that keeps time accurately? If you have salvaged a modern battery-clock mechanism from your take-it-apart experiments ("Inventing Backwards"), try using that to make a new, useful, or just goofy clock.

Naturalize it

Snap it. Many cameras today are very complex and expensive. But you can take pictures with nothing more than a cardboard box and unexposed film. With a pinhole in one end of a box and the film in the other, you can take a picture. There is no quick film advance or fancy light metering system. Just guess what the exposure time should be, and see how your pictures develop. Pinhole cameras work best when there is lots of light. Try holding the camera very still. When you have mastered the technique, try moving the camera slightly to see what effects you get.

Heat it up. If you live in a sunny climate, try making a solar oven. Can you focus enough of the sun's energy on one spot to boil a cup of water, or cook a hot dog?

Measure it

One thing that interests everyone is the weather. You can't invent a way to change the weather, but you can develop ways to measure it and predict it.

Design a weather gauge. Rain gauges are pretty straightforward. A wind gauge is not. And what about a sun gauge—can you make an electronic thermometer? You will need parts from an electronics supply store. How about a homemade barometer?

Once you have your weather instruments set up, compare your readings to the ones reported on the radio or in the newspaper. Are there consistent differences that might indicate your area is warmer or cooler, wetter or drier, than where they take their official measurements?

Keep records to see if you can learn what wind, temperature, and cloud patterns predict different weather conditions. Then see if you can beat the professional forecasters. If you can devise a simple and accurate prediction method, many people will be interested in learning about it.

KEEP TINKERING

These are only a few of the ideas that other people have come up with. Now it's your turn to invent some new ones Start tinkering, and have fun!

MAKING YOUR INVENTIONS PAY OFF

How can your inventions pay off? There are several ways.
While you are inventing, you are having fun—and learning more than you realize. Inventing helps you to be creative and curious, and it helps you learn new skills. That's the best payoff. But there are others.

INVENTION CONTESTS

You could enter your invention in a contest. See if your school has a science fair or an invention convention. If not, maybe you could help start one.

You can also compete at the regional or national level in some contests. You may be able to compete even if your school doesn't have a contest. The following list tells about a few contests, the grade levels for each, and their deadlines. Since each contest has its own rules, and since each could change the deadline, contact the contest-holders directly to get up-to-date information. Your school might have the information already—talk to the gifted and talented coordinator or the school counseling office.

Grades	Contest and address	Deadlines and other data
1–6	Invention Convention Silver Burdett and Ginn 250 James Street Morristown, NJ 07960	February 15
K–8	Invent America U.S. Patent Model Foundation 510 King Street, Suite 420 Alexandria, VA 22314	April (Your school must join.)
K–8	Weekly Reader National Invention Contest 245 Long Hill Road Middletown, CT 06457	Mid-December
9–12	Duracell NSTA Scholarship Competition Inventions using batteries National Science Teachers Association 1742 Connecticut Avenue NW Washington, D.C. 20009	December
College	B.F. Goodrich Collegiate Inventors Program National Invention Center 80 W. Bowery Street Akron, OH 44308	December 31 (Most entrants are graduate students.)

SELLING YOUR INVENTION

Someday, you may have a truly great idea that could become a product. Before you rush into it, you should know that most inventions never make money for their inventors. Only one or two patented inventions out of a hundred earns a profit. A few inventions do spectacularly well, some bring in a little profit, and most never get produced or never sell.

But if you are convinced that you have a money-making invention, here are some things you might do.

Protect your idea

There is less swiping of ideas than most people think. But it does occur, and you should give your ideas the best protection you can afford. Here's where your inventor's log is useful. If you have chronicled the invention process in your notebook, indicating dates, and have had witnesses sign it, you are in a much better position to defend your ideas in court. Having a "notary public" sign your log is also a good idea.

Do you need more protection? It depends. If you are really serious, you might want to talk to a patent attorney. You can find one listed in the yellow pages of the phone book. For a fee, an attorney can tell you about patents, copyrights, and trademarks. Make sure you understand how much each will cost and how long it will take.

Sell your idea

Identify the companies that make the product you have improved, or identify the companies that make products closely related to the one you have invented. These companies will be the ones most interested in your new or improved product. Some companies rely solely on their own staffs for creative ideas, and may not talk to you. Keep trying until you find one that is interested in the possibility of buying your idea.

An alternative approach is to use an agent to sell your invention. The agent will take a percentage of your royalties, but will have contacts within the business community and will know how to sell your invention. You can ask a patent attorney to help you find an agent.

Warning: There are several rip-off invention submission companies in operation. Typically, you hear their ads on the radio. Be careful. Check with the State Attorney General's office and the Better Business Bureau to see what complaints have been filed against them. Since almost every company has had some complaints, look to see how they resolved the complaints. Also ask the company for a list of prior clients and business references you can call. Then do call these references. This procedure will take you only a few hours and a few dollars of telephone charges, and it could save you from making a big mistake.

Make it yourself

In most cases, becoming a manufacturer yourself is not the best approach. However, if you have the capability to make the product and to distribute it to stores or to sell it yourself, you might consider this. Estimate how

PATENTS: ONLY FOR THE SERIOUS

Patents are useful, but they are expensive too. Getting a patent could easily cost $5,000. You won't want to spend that much unless you are convinced that your invention will earn you lots more money than that.

If you want to know more about patents, you can get information at your library, join an inventors group, or talk to a patent attorney. You can find patent attorneys listed in the yellow pages of the telephone book. It may take several phone calls to locate a local inventors group. Start by asking patent attorneys or the information desk of your public library. Some groups are listed in inventor magazines. Also look in your local newspaper for listings of club meetings.

many items you will be able to sell, and see if you can make that number. Is it worth your time to manufacture products, or would you rather let someone else do it for you?

If you want to start making products, there may be financial and consulting help available to you. Check in your city to see if they offer loans or grants to new, small businesses. Also see if there is an "incubator" in your area. Incubators are supported by cities to encourage new businesses that will bring prosperity to the area.

See if you have a local SCORE chapter—that stands for Service Corps of Retired Executives. If there's one in your area, these retired volunteers can be a great help to you in setting up a business. And, they don't charge.

If you are working on inventions that involve toys or games, look at the Levy and Weingartner book, *Inside Santa's Workshop.* It has lots of information on that industry.

For general information on the patent system, you can get a videotape and booklet, called *A Patently Good Idea,* from the National Invention Center.

Also, find out if there is an inventor's club in your area. The information desk at the library may have some information for you. Typically, these clubs are filled with people who have experience with marketing their ideas and would like to help you.

Sell your written ideas

If you decide not to make your invention, and not to sell it to a manufacturer, you still could earn money with your ideas. Many magazines have columns on hobbies, with written pieces that are submitted by readers. Some of these magazines pay for new ideas. Others may give free subscriptions to people who submit ideas. Try selling your ideas to these magazines. Ask a librarian to help you find magazines that might be interested in hearing about your inventions.

Regardless of what you do with your inventions, you are a winner. It is the process of inventing, even more than the products, that make inventing valuable.

Keep asking questions and seeking answers. Keep trying new approaches. Keep solving problems. Keep on inventing. Good luck.

BOOKS AND MAGAZINES FOR INVENTORS

Caney, Steven. *Invention Book.* New York: Workman Publishing, 1985.

Flack, Jerry D. *Inventing, Inventions, and Inventors. A Teaching Resource Book.* Englewood, Colo.: Teacher Ideas Press, 1989.

Herbert, Don. *Mr. Wizard's Supermarket Science.* New York: Random House, 1980.

Kukes, Roger. *The Zoetrope Book.* Portland, Ore.: Klassroom Kinetics, 1985.

Levy, Richard C. and Ronald O. Weingartner. *Inside Santa's Workshop.* New York: Henry Holt, 1990.

Macaulay, David. *The Way Things Work.* Boston: Houghton Mifflin, 1988.

Renner, Al. *How to Build a Better Mousetrap Car.* New York: Dodd, Mead, 1977.

Shafer, Kathryn E. and Thomas B. Hollingsworth. *A Patently Good Idea.* A videotape and teacher's guide. Akron, Ohio: The National Invention Center, 1990.

Shlesinger, B. Edward, Jr. *How to Invent: A Text for Teachers and Students.* New York: IFI/Plenum, 1987.

Stanish, Bob. *The Unconventional Invention Book: Classroom Activities for Activating Student Inventiveness.* Carthage, Ill.: Good Apple, 1981.

Weiss, Stephen. *Wings and Things: Origami That Flies.* New York: St. Martin's Press, 1984.

Zubrowski, Bernie. *Balloons: Building and Experimenting with Inflatable Toys.* New York: Morrow Junior Books, 1990.

Zubrowski, Bernie. *Blinkers and Buzzers: Building and Experimenting with Electricity and Magnetism.* New York: Morrow Junior Books, 1991.

Zubrowski, Bernie. *Clocks: Building and Experimenting with Model Timepieces.* New York: Beech Tree Books, 1988.

Zubrowski, Bernie. *Messing Around with Drinking Straw Construction.* Boston: Little, Brown, 1981.

Zubrowski, Bernie. *Messing Around with Water Pumps and Siphons.* Boston: Little, Brown, 1981.

Zubrowski, Bernie. *Raceways: Having Fun with Balls and Tracks.* New York: William Morrow, 1985.

Zubrowski, Bernie. *Tops: Building and Experimenting with Spinning Toys.* New York: Morrow Junior Books, 1989.

Inventors Digest
2132 E. Bijou St.
Colorado Springs, CO 80909-5950

Invent Magazine
Box 6664
Woodland Hills, CA 97365

Ties Magazine
College of Design Arts
Drexel University
Philadelphia, PA 19104